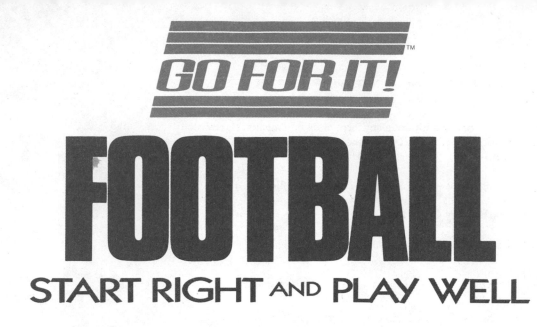

GO FOR IT! ™

FOOTBALL

START RIGHT AND PLAY WELL

by Bill Gutman

with Illustrations by Ben Brown

MARSHALL CAVENDISH
CORPORATION

GREY CASTLE PRESS

Marshall Cavendish Edition, Freeport, New York.

Published by arrangement with Grey Castle Press, Lakeville, Ct.

Printed in the USA

The Library of Congress Cataloging in Publication Data

Gutman, Bill.
    Football : start right and play well / by Bill Gutman ; with
illustrations by Ben Brown.
        p.   cm. — (Go for it!)
    ''Published by arrangement with Grey Castle Press, Lakeville, Ct.''—
T.p. verso.
    Summary: Describes the history and current teams, leagues, and
championships of football and provides instruction on how to play
the game.
    ISBN 0-942545-85-0 (lib. bdg.)
    1. Football—Juvenile literature. [1. Football.] I. Brown,
Ben, 1921–   Ill. II. Title. III. Series: Gutman, Bill. Go for
it!
GV950.7.G87   1990
796.332—dc20   89-7585
                                                            CIP
                                                             AC

Photo credits: Culver Pictures, page 6; Focus On Sports, page 10; UPI/Bettmann, pages 7 and 9.

Special thanks to: Carl Ferraro, varsity football coach, Pawling High School, Pawling, N.Y.

Picture research: Omni Photo Communications, Inc.

ABOUT THE AUTHOR

Bill Gutman is the author of over 70 books for children and young adults. The majority of his titles have dealt with sports, in both fiction and non-fiction, including ''how-to'' books. His name is well-known to librarians who make it their business to be informed about books of special interest to boys and reluctant readers. He lives in Poughquag, New York.

ABOUT THE ILLUSTRATOR

Ben Brown's experience ranges from cartoonist to gallery painter. He is a graduate of the High School of Music & Art in New York City and the University of Iowa Art School. He has been a member of the National Academy of Design and the Art Students' League. He has illustrated government training manuals for the disadvantaged (using sports as themes), and his animation work for the American Bible Society won two blue ribbons from the American Film Festival. He lives in Great Barrington, Massachusetts.

In order to keep the instructions in this book as simple as possible, the author has chosen in most cases to use ''he'' to signify both boys and girls.

A BRIEF HISTORY

It took football many years to become the sport it is today. In the early days of America, boys would sometimes play a game using a pig's bladder as a ball. They would form two teams, and each would try to push, kick or shove the ball through the other team to a goal. More often, the teams would kick, push and shove each other.

It was out of these rough and tumble games that football was born. The game used some skills from the sport of soccer, and others from rugby. The big difference between these two games is that in rugby a player can pick the ball up and run with it.

Many feel that the first game of American football was played in November of 1875 between Harvard and Yale Universities. But that game hardly looked like football of today. The man who really shaped the modern game of football was Walter Camp. He started changing the game while he was at Yale University in 1880.

The first thing Camp did was reduce the number of players on a side to 11, the same number that play today. But that wasn't all. Camp also made the field smaller and then suggested a rule that would allow the center to ''snap'' the ball before each play. That started the modern line of scrimmage. It also allowed teams to plan their plays in advance.

A short time later, Camp decided to draw chalk lines five yards apart on the field, making it easier to measure how far the ball moved on each play. It also led to the nickname for a football field—the gridiron.

Notre Dame's Knute Rockne was one of the great pioneers in football. He helped to make the pass a strong offensive weapon.

As the rules changed, more colleges began playing the sport. And, slowly, the game began taking shape. Not too many teams or players used helmets before 1897. That year, Coach Glenn "Pop" Warner equipped his Carlisle Indian football team with headgear. Soon all college football players were wearing helmets.

By the turn of the century, professional football teams were turning up here and there. There were no leagues then, and teams would just play other nearby clubs or rivals across the state. One of the great early pro rivalries was between the Canton Bulldogs and the Massillon Tigers. These teams were from nearby cities in Ohio, and their rivalry continued for a long time. In fact, Canton is now the site of the Pro Football Hall of Fame.

There wasn't much passing in the early days of football. One reason was that the old ball was round and fat, which made it difficult to grip. Instead, the game was geared to power running and hard blocking. Knute Rockne and a teammate named Gus Dorais showed how the pass could work when their Notre Dame team upset mighty Army in 1913. Rockne would later become one of Notre Dame's greatest coaches.

It was really the professional teams who made the pass a great football weapon. This happened after the beginning of the National Football League in 1920. One of the men who helped start the NFL was George Halas. He had a team in Chicago called the Staleys, but pretty soon the name was changed to the Chicago Bears, the same team that plays in the NFL today.

Most of football's early stars were great runners. The first was Jim Thorpe, who played under Pop Warner at the Carlisle Indian

Jim Thorpe was another of the game's early heroes. Here, he is in the uniform of the Canton Bulldogs in 1921.

School. A full-blooded Indian, Thorpe was one of the greatest athletes of all-time. He could play any sport, but football was his favorite. When he left college in 1915, he joined the Canton Bulldogs to begin his pro career.

Jim Thorpe had a great career and helped bring more fans to the young league. Following Thorpe was another great college runner. His name was Harold "Red" Grange, and he played for the University of Illinois. When Grange became a pro with the Chicago Bears in 1925, fans from all over flocked to see him. He helped the young league grow even more.

Another great runner from the 1930s was Bronko Nagurski. He was a huge fullback who ran over people. Pro football was still a rough-and-tumble game then, and Nagurski played just that way.

In the late 1930s and into the 1940s, pro football teams began to throw the ball more often. Arnie Herber of Green Bay was one of the better passing quarterbacks of the time. But the two men who really made the pass game work were Sid Luckman of the Bears and Slingin' Sammy Baugh of the Redskins. Luckman was the first quarterback to operate from the T formation, and Baugh was the first to throw for big yardage.

In the 1950s, pro football really came of age. Another fullback, Jim Brown from Syracuse University, joined the Cleveland Browns in 1957. He is still thought by many to be the greatest running back of all time. He was followed by the likes of Gale Sayers, O.J. Simpson, Walter Payton, Tony Dorsett and Eric Dickerson. They are some of the best.

There were also great quarterbacks coming into the league in the 1950s. Such players as Bobby Layne, Bob Waterfield , Norm Van Brocklin, John Unitas, Sonny Jurgensen, Y.A. Tittle, Joe Namath, Roger Staubach, Fran Tarkenton, Terry Bradshaw, Dan Fouts, Dan Marino and John Elway have all left their mark on the pro game.

Jim Brown started his career in the 1950s. Many people think he was the game's greatest running back.

The first Super Bowl was played in 1967 and won by the Green Bay Packers, who were coached by the legendary Vince Lombardi. Today, the Super Bowl is one of the great sporting events, and pro football is a huge business.

John Elway is one of pro football's leading quarterbacks. Here, he is looking for a Denver receiver.

In fact, there have been too many great players and coaches to name here. It took pro football a long time to become as popular as major league baseball. But it happened, thanks to the great pioneer players like Thorpe, Grange and others who played through those tough early days.

ORGANIZED FOOTBALL

Football today is a game played at many different levels. Youngsters can begin playing Pop Warner football at an early age. If they are good enough, they can keep playing. Then comes high school football, college and finally the pros.

Of course, anyone can have fun with a football by getting a group together and finding an open field. Some like to play "touch" football, a fast game that isn't too rough. Instead of tackling a runner or receiver, the players simply touch him. It is possible to play touch and still learn the skills of running, passing, blocking and receiving.

If a young person wants to play tackle, he should play in a real league. That way, he will have good equipment and learn to play the game the right way. Football is a very rough game, and it's important to learn all the skills. Otherwise, a player can get hurt very easily.

Today there are programs for all ages. A good Pop Warner coach can teach kids how the game is played. There are Pop Warner League programs all over the country. Junior high and high school programs are also everywhere. There are many places where the whole town loves its high school football team.

The best high school players will then go on to play football in college. College football today is bigger than ever. Teams play in huge stadiums before thousands and thousands of people. Many games are on television, and the best teams get to play in the special Bowl games at the end of the season.

Even the smaller colleges play football. They play against other schools of the same size. Their teams aren't on television as often as the teams from big schools. But the fact that there are so many teams shows just how popular the game has become.

By the 1980s, the National Football League had grown to 28 teams. They are split into six divisions and two conferences. The American Conference and National Conference both have 14 teams. Each conference has an eastern, central and western division, and each team plays 16 games during the regular season.

Ten of the 28 teams now make it to the play-offs. After an elimination game in each conference, there are semifinals and then conference finals. The two conference winners then go to the Super Bowl, where they play for the world championship.

The Super Bowl is watched by millions of people all over the country. It is as big a sports spectacle as the World Series in baseball. Many of the top NFL players earn a great deal of money and are well-known sports figures.

For many people, the sport of football has become a big part of their lives.

LEARNING THE GAME

Playing Football

There are some basic things a young person should know before he plays football. Games take place on a flat field with chalk lines five yards apart. A standard field is 100 yards long from goal line to goal line. It is 53⅓ yards wide. There is a 10-yard area called the end zone behind each goal line. The goalposts are at the back of the end zones. The crossbar on each post is 10 feet off the ground, while the vertical posts are 18½ feet apart.

Players in Pop Warner football may find themselves on a smaller field. But once a player reaches high school, he will play on a standard field.

The object of the game is to take the ball from any point on the field across the opponent's goal line. A team crossing its opponent's goal line scores a touchdown. A touchdown counts for six points. The team then has a chance to try for one or two extra points. If the team decides to kick the ball through the goalposts, it counts for one extra point. If they decide to run or pass the ball across the goal line, it counts for two extra points.

The offensive team always tries to move the ball toward the opponent's goal line. The defensive team tries to stop the offense from moving the ball. If a defensive team can stop the offense, then that team's offense takes over the ball.

There are 11 players in the game for each team at the same

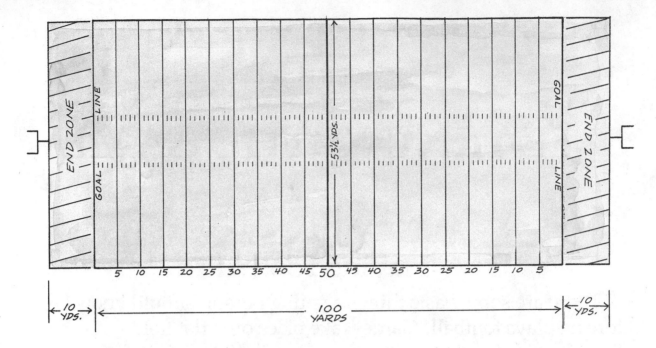

This is the standard football field, or gridiron. The field is 100 yards long, with lines marked every five yards. The end zones are ten yards deep, and the goalposts are on the back line of the end zone. The field is 53⅓ yards wide. Young players just beginning the game may play on a smaller field.

time. Most football teams, however, have more than 40 players on the squad. In the pros and at most colleges, there are different players for offense and for defense. At small colleges and high schools, some players will play both offense and defense.

Offensive teams try to move the ball by running or passing. A running game always needs several good runners, or ballcarriers. Some must be fast and shifty. These runners can get past tacklers with good fakes and ''moves'' and then outrun them once they get into the clear. Other runners must be big and strong so they can run through the line and drive hard for extra yardage.

Runners also need blockers. It is the linemen who must block the defenders to make a running game work. The runner without the ball must often block for the ballcarrier as well. Like everything else in football, a good running game is the result of team effort.

14

The passing game is also a team effort. A team must have a good passer to throw the ball to his receivers. And the receivers must know how to get into the open to catch the ball. Once a receiver catches the ball, he becomes a ballcarrier. So he must know how to run as well.

Like the running game, the passing game cannot work without blocking. The linemen and backs must block for the passer. They

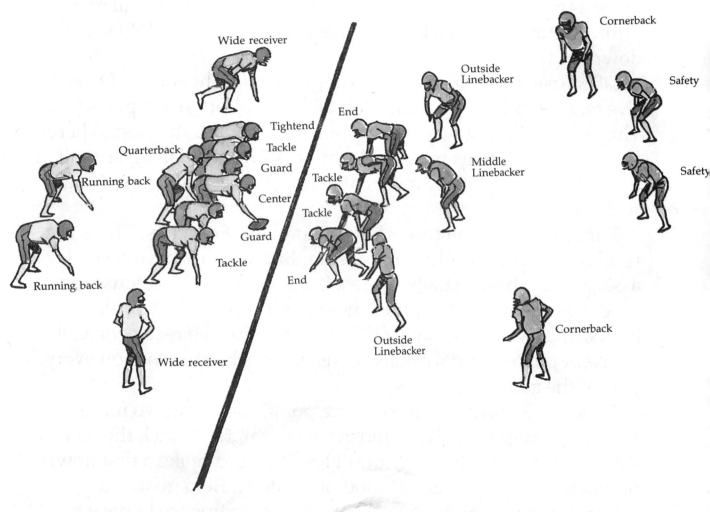

This is just one basic football alignment. The team on the left is the offense. The quarterback is ready to take the snap from center. He has two running backs behind him and two wide receivers split out from the line. There are five linemen and the tight end along the line. The defense has four linemen, three linebackers and four deep defensive backs. But there are many other offenses and defenses football teams can use.

must keep the defensive players from getting to him, so he will have enough time to find his receiver and throw the ball to him.

The offensive team has four "downs" in which to make at least 10 yards. If they make 10 yards or more, they get a first down and start over again. If they fail to make 10 yards in four downs, the other team gets the football at that spot on the field.

However, if a team has a fourth-down play and feels it cannot make a first down, it can kick the football away. This is called a punt. A punt enables a team to give the ball up, but a lot farther downfield.

Of course, the game is not as simple as it might sound. Defensive teams work very hard to stop all kinds of offensive plays. They have different ways of stopping the run and the pass. Therefore, offensive teams must find ways to move the ball against all kinds of defenses. They must come up with a "game plan" that will work.

That's why football teams have a number of coaches. There is a head coach who runs the entire team. But he must have several assistant coaches. Usually, one assistant handles the offense, another the defense. Sometimes there is a coach for the running backs, another for the line and still another for the receivers. College and pro teams have many assistant coaches to work on every part of the game.

Besides the touchdown and extra point, there are two more ways to score points. The offensive team can try to kick the ball through the uprights if they don't feel they can make a first down or touchdown. If the kick is good, it's called a field goal and counts for three points. All college and pro teams try to have a good field goal kicker on the squad.

The other way to score is to tackle the offensive team's ballcarrier behind his own goal line. That is called a safety and is worth two points. So while touchdowns give a team the most points at

A good coach is the best thing that can happen to a young player. The coach will teach the fundamentals of the game, devise the game strategy and tell each player just what he has to do.

once, many games have been won and lost on a field goal or safety.

A good football player will learn about all parts of the game. He may want to play a position on offense, but he should still know about defense. That's why it is good for a beginning player to learn a few different positions. He should try playing both offense and defense. In the long run, that will make him a better player.

Getting Ready To Play

Football is not an easy game to play because it is very physical. A player is often blocking, hitting or tackling, or being hit or tackled on every play. To do this play after play takes a lot of desire and heart. It also takes a player who keeps himself in good condition and is always ready for action.

Anyone who wants to play football must start even before practice begins. Once he decides to play, he must begin to get in shape. Running is the best way for a person to build up his wind so he doesn't get tired during a game. The quarterback, running backs, receivers, linebackers and defensive backs will all run a great deal during a game. So a regular running program before the season starts will really help.

Football players must also be strong. So it is important to work out. Exercises like pull-ups, push-ups and sit-ups are very helpful. Lifting weights to become stronger is even more effective. But a young person should work with someone who can show him the right way. To work with weights without knowing about them could hurt more than help.

Besides regular running, it is also helpful to run quick sprints. That means a player should run 10 or 15 yards as fast as possible. Then he can rest or walk for a few seconds before sprinting again. There will be many times during a football game when a sudden burst of speed is important. By training this way, a player will always be ready to turn on the speed for a short distance.

In a way, it is also important for a player to get his mind ready. Football is a sport that includes a lot of hard hitting. A player must be ready to both dish it out and take it. Hitting can sometimes lead to bumps and bruises, or even injuries, and a player must know this ahead of time. Of course, good equipment and proper training reduce the chances of injuries. If a young person

18

Getting in shape is a big part of playing football. One of the best things a football player can do is run wind sprints. This means running very hard for 10 or 15 yards, stopping for a few seconds, then sprinting again. A football player often needs these bursts of speed during a game.

Other exercises, such as push-ups and sit-ups, are also very important. Football players must be strong to play an entire game. A good coach will always give his players a whole list of exercises to do.

is always worrying about getting hurt, he can't be the best football player possible. And he won't help his team that way.

For these reasons, it is important to be ready for football before starting to play. If a player gets in shape and prepares as well as he can, he will have a better chance to make the team and see action.

Choosing A Position

Choosing a position is a decision that will usually be made by the coach. He will give out positions by size, weight, toughness, speed and the ability to perform certain skills. Sometimes it helps if a person knows which position he wants to play. But knowing what it takes to play each position will help even more.

The quarterback is the hub of the offense. Each play begins when he takes the snap from the center. A quarterback must be smart and a natural leader. He has to want to take charge in crucial situations, at crunch time. And he has to have a number of other skills.

To begin with, a quarterback must be cool under pressure. On pass plays, he must be able to look downfield for his receivers and not worry about the defenders who are trying to get to him. He also should have a good throwing arm and must be able to run. And he has to follow the plays and game plan set up by the coach.

Running backs must be tough and courageous. They go into every game knowing they will be hit nearly every time they carry the ball. They have to be able to keep going at top speed, no matter what. The smaller running backs must be fast and agile; the bigger ones must be tough and willing to run head first into the line. It helps to have a runner's instinct. This means knowing where to run and cut in a split second, without really thinking.

Pass receivers must be fast, too. They have to use their quickness to get into the open. This means having many moves and being able to fake defensive backs. They must also have "good hands" to catch all kinds of passes—high, low, hard and soft. And they must be tough enough to block and to take hard hits after they catch the ball.

Offensive linemen are bigger and not as fast as the runners and receivers. They must be able to use their size to block on both running and passing plays. Linemen usually aren't as well known as quarterbacks or running backs, but they are just as important. No team can win without a solid line. So a lineman should never feel that he isn't a big part of a football squad.

Defensive linemen are generally big and strong, and they must have a lot of skills. A good lineman has to use his head because a defensive line must stop the rushing game and try to get to the quarter-back. Any person thinking of playing the defensive line should remember that his job can be a big part of winning a football game.

Linebackers have a very tough job. Sometimes they have to play right on the line. So they must be strong enough to take on an offensive lineman. But other times they will have to cover a pass receiver. So they must be fast enough to keep up with him. Still other times they will find themselves chasing a runner. So a linebacker must be smart. He must be able to "read" a play very quickly. This means he must see where the play is going and decide just how he will handle it. If he makes the wrong decision, the whole team can be hurt.

Defensive backs must be quick and tough. Cornerbacks do not have to be big, but they must be aggressive. They have to be tough enough to fight off blocks and tackle ballcarriers. They must also cover the fastest of pass receivers, many times one-on-one. Every once in a while, they may have to gamble on an interception. If they miss, it can mean a touchdown for the offense.

The safeties must do many of the same things as the corner-

Almost anyone can play football. A young person just beginning should try to find the position that is best for him. As a rule, smaller players are usually **quarterbacks, runners, pass receivers** or **defensive backs.** The bigger players are **linemen** and **linebackers,** and maybe even **tight ends.**

backs. They usually are a little bigger because they sometimes come right up on the line to charge or ''blitz'' the quarterback. It is the safeties who usually cover the biggest pass receiver, the tight end. The safety is also the last line of defense, so he must be ready to make the big tackle at any time.

Obviously, every position on a football team is important. Whether a youngster plays offense or defense, he can play a big part in winning *or* losing.

Football is a total team sport. No one or two players can win a game all by themselves. It takes everyone playing together and playing hard. And that's the way it has always been.

Equipment

Just a word about equipment. Because football is a contact sport, players are well protected by special equipment. There is a helmet to protect against head and neck injuries. Helmets today also have face masks to protect the players' faces.

All players will wear shoulder pads which strap on under the jersey. They can also extend down to protect part of the rib cage. Hip and thigh pads are built into an undergarment that the players step into. A player should be sure to wear a cup to protect the groin area. Knee pads can also be worn under the regular football pants.

The helmet may be the most important piece of equipment a football player has. Today's helmets protect not only the head, but also the face and eyes. They are designed by experts and can cost a great deal of money. Every player should also wear a mouthpiece to protect his teeth.

The football uniform (right) covers up a great deal of the protective padding a player wears. The player on the left shows the shoulder pads, rib protectors, thigh and knee pads. He also has his ankles taped to prevent sprains. It is very important to have the right equipment when playing the game.

For added protection, some players tape their ankles and wear hand and wrist pads. Linemen will often wear these, but the backs and ends need their hands to be free.

There are also other pieces of equipment that protect injured players. Doctors have made special knee braces and jackets to cushion knee and rib injuries. Some pro players wear these so they can keep playing. However, a youngster just learning the game would not be allowed to play with injuries.

Learning To Be
A Quarterback

Quarterback may be the most important position on a football team because the quarterback gets the ball from the center to begin every single play on offense. A good quarterback is a confident leader who can execute all the plays the coach puts into the playbook.

This means he must be able to hand off smoothly to his running backs. He must also be able to drop back to pass, or roll to his right or left on option plays. An option play allows the quarterback to either run or throw, and he has to decide which option will work better. He will often have to decide in a split second. That takes a lot of practice and experience.

The very first thing a new quarterback must learn is to take the snap from his center. The center passes the ball between his legs directly into the quarterback's hands. This sounds simple, but it

A quarterback must work well with his center because each play begins with the snap. The center must pass the ball back between his legs to the quarterback. Both players must practice this basic pass very often until it becomes almost automatic for them.

takes practice. The quarterback calls signals, meaning the center will snap it on a certain count, or number. If he snaps too late, the quarterback may be already moving away and will drop it.

The quarterback must spend time with his center, practicing counts and snaps. On straight handoffs, the quarterback will turn either to his right or left and place the ball right into the belly of his running back. The runner is already moving quickly toward the line, so the timing must be just right. Sometimes the quarterback will fake to one runner and then give to ball to another. Again, the quarterback must work together with his center and running backs to get the timing just right.

There are also times when the quarterback will "pitch out" to a runner. Instead of handing the ball directly to the runner, the

The quarterback must also practice handing off to his running backs. To do this well takes almost perfect timing between the two players. When the quarterback turns, the runner should be right there to take the ball with both hands. And the quarterback must place the football almost in the runner's belly.

quarterback will flip the ball underhanded to his running back. The pitchout may travel from five to 10 feet, and the quarterback must learn to lead the runner. This means he must flip the ball to where the back will be when the ball gets there. Otherwise, the pitchout will wind up behind the fast-moving back.

Ball handling is a big part of the running game, and the quarterback must be good at it. In fact, there will be times when he will take a running play and pretend to hand the ball to his back. But then he will take it back and look downfield to pass. That's called a play-action fake.

In today's football, passing is perhaps the most important thing a quarterback must do. It takes a great deal of practice to become a good passing quarterback. To begin with, a quarterback must know the right grip and correct throwing motion.

A very young quarterback may start with a smaller football so he can learn the right grip and motion from the beginning. To start, he should spread his fingers as far apart as he can and then lay them across the laces of the ball. The little finger should press hard on the laces, and so should the finger next to it. The middle finger should be just above the laces and the index finger across the seam near the tip. The thumb should be curled as far as possible around the outside of the ball.

If the ball is being gripped the right way, there will be a little space between the quarterback's palm and the ball. When he releases the ball, it should roll off his fingertips. The index finger is the last finger off the ball. It will help keep the nose of the ball up and give it a tight spiral, making it much easier to catch.

The football should be thrown with an overhand motion. When the quarterback gets ready to pass, the ball should be up at ear level. He should keep his nonpassing hand on it as a guide. In some ways, the passing motion will be similar to the motion of a pitcher throwing a baseball.

A quarterback must use the right grip when throwing the football. His pinky and ring finger should grip the laces tightly. The second finger should be just above the laces and the index finger up near the end of the ball. The fingers should also be spread as far apart as they can. With this grip, a good quarterback will be able to throw a spiral when he passes.

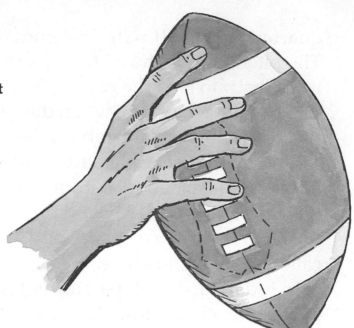

On a pass play, the quarterback begins by taking the snap from the center. He then drops back so his blockers can form a protective "pocket" around him. When dropping back, the quarterback should always look downfield and be ready to pass.

When the quarterback sees his target, he brings his arm back from ear level to behind his head. He then steps into the throw. A right-handed passer will step with his left foot. A left-handed passer will step with his right foot. As he starts to throw, he will lead with his hip and waist. This way he won't be throwing with only his arm.

As he turns his hips in the direction of the throw, his arm follows. The throw should be directly overhand, with the arm snapping it off at the release point, which should be up high. As he follows through, the passer should bring his arm straight down, not across his body. This motion will assure a straight throw.

Once in the pocket, the quarterback must find his receivers quickly. This means he must know their pass patterns and must also see how closely they are covered by the defenders. That's why the quarterback must keep the ball chest high, ready to throw. That way, when he spots an open receiver, he can release the ball quickly.

The grip and motion are only the beginning. The basic throw should be practiced as much as possible. Once he can throw the ball well, the quarterback can start working on his team's passing game.

Of course, there are a number of other basic things to learn. To begin with, on passing plays, the quarterback will usually drop back. This means taking three to seven steps backward very quickly. Some quarterbacks prefer to backpedal. Others retreat sideways. But by dropping back, the quarterback is giving his re-

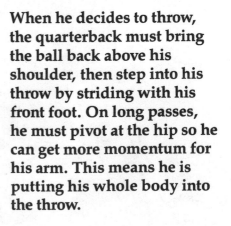

When he decides to throw, the quarterback must bring the ball back above his shoulder, then step into his throw by striding with his front foot. On long passes, he must pivot at the hip so he can get more momentum for his arm. This means he is putting his whole body into the throw.

ceivers a chance to run downfield. He is also giving his blockers time to set up a ''pocket'' around him.

The blocking pocket allows the quarterback time to throw. Once in the pocket, the quarterback must get used to looking downfield and finding his receivers quickly. If one receiver is covered, he must find another. If all are covered, he has to run or scramble. Maybe a receiver can get into the open during that time.

The quarterback must work closely with his receivers. If he learns their moves, he will have a better chance of knowing where

Most good quarterbacks throw with a direct, over-hand motion. This makes it harder for a lineman to block the pass and allows the quarterback to get more ''zip'' on the ball. He must also follow through with his arm by bringing it straight down, not across his body.

they'll be at all times. And he will also know what kind of pass to throw.

Some passes have to be thrown hard and on a line. Others must be lofted over the defense and float into the receiver's hands. And a few have to be thrown to a spot, meaning the ball and receiver will get there at the same time.

No matter what kind of pass a quarterback throws, he must be accurate. He must be able to throw the ball just where he wants it.

A quarterback must also learn to "lead" his receiver. This means throwing the football to the spot the receiver will be when the ball comes down. To do this, a quarterback must know the speed of his receiver. He must also decide whether to loft the ball high or throw it low and on a line. That's why quarterbacks must practice their passing for many long hours.

Quarterbacks sometimes practice throwing the football through a car tire hanging on a rope from a tree. When they get good enough, they swing the tire back and forth and try to throw the ball through it.

The most important part of passing is knowing how to lead a receiver. This means throwing to the spot where the receiver will be. And since receivers are often very fast, a quarterback will sometimes be throwing to a spot quite a distance from where the receiver is when he starts to throw. It isn't easy, but all it takes is practice.

Learning To Be
A Running Back

Speed, quickness and power are the things a running back needs the most. The really great ones often have all three. But other very good runners only have one or two. The trick is learning to make the most of what you've got.

The smaller, fast running backs will often run outside. This means they will run toward the sidelines, hoping to pick up blocks and get into the clear. The bigger, stronger runners often run inside, through the middle of the line. They get the "tough" yards that way. But many are often fast and shifty enough to make big gains once they get through the line.

Vince Lombardi, the great pro coach of the Green Bay Packers, once said that the good back always "runs to daylight." This means a runner must find the hole in the line and burst through it very quickly. In fact, the quick burst of speed is one of the best tools a runner can have.

There are some basic skills that every running back must know. First of all, every runner must know the team's plays very well.

A good running back will be able to find a ''hole'' opened by his offensive line. When the runner sees a hole, he must burst through it as fast as he can. If he doesn't get through quickly, the defense will close it up.

When the coach or quarterback calls a play, the runner must know exactly what to do. If the play calls for him to get the ball, he has to know how each lineman will block on the play and where to run to find the hole.

Some plays call for the runner to go ''off tackle,'' others over the center. Still others call for him to run outside. So as soon as the play is called, he must know where to go, with or without the ball.

When taking a handoff from the quarterback, a running back

Runners must also learn to follow their blockers. This means running behind the blockers, then watching to see which way the blocker will move the defensive man. If the blocker moves the defender to the left, the runner must be ready to burst quickly to the right.

will make a kind of pocket with his arms. He does this by raising the arm closest to the quarterback across his chest. He keeps his other arm level across his stomach. He will also keep the fingers on both hands spread. Then the quarterback will place the ball right in his stomach, and the runner will close his hands on it, one from above and one from below.

If the runner is going directly into the line, he should keep both hands on the ball because defenders can slap and grab at it. They will try to make him fumble. He should keep both hands on the

In heavy traffic, a running back must always hold the ball with two hands. Defensive players will try to grab or slap the ball to make the runner drop it. If he fumbles, it's a free ball and anyone can grab it.

ball because defenders can slap and grab at it. He should stay low to the ground and keep his head down. But he must also be able to see any holes that have opened and be ready to burst through them.

If the runner gets into the open field, he can carry the ball with one arm. But he should still keep it tucked close to his body with his hand and forearm. He should never carry it away from his body with his hand. It's too easy to lose it that way.

A good runner seems to have the instincts to make the right moves. But all runners should practice their moves. For example, in a one-on-one situation, a runner can try to get past a tackler by faking one way, then going another. Or he can make a sharp cut by planting one leg, pushing off and going the other way. Runners can practice all these fakes and cuts by working with teammates.

Sometimes, when a runner is hit by a tackler, he can suddenly spin and pull free. The more he carries the football, the more ways he will find to get away from tacklers.

In today's game, runners must also block for the quarterback or for their fellow running backs. And they must be ready to catch passes. Therefore, a running back should also pay attention to learning how to block and how to catch passes. A final piece of advice to the runner—always run hard. If you're going to be hit, make sure you keep going forward and don't back off from the contact. Hang on to that football until you hear the whistle blow. And, above all, always run to daylight.

Learning To Be
A Pass Receiver

Even the best of quarterbacks will not have a good day passing if he doesn't have good pass receivers. He needs receivers who can run pass patterns, catch the football and then turn upfield and make some more yardage.

There are two types of pass receivers. The first are called wide receivers or wide outs. They usually line up wide of the line of scrimmage on either the right or left side. As a rule, they are fast and have good moves. Wide receivers need speed and moves to get free of the defensive backs who guard them.

The other pass receiver is the tight end. He plays on the line of scrimmage outside of one of the tackles. The tight end will sometimes block on running plays and will also catch passes. Tight

Pass receivers must know how to run good patterns and get into the open. And they must also have good, "soft" hands to catch the ball when it reaches them. Receivers should always spread their fingers wide open and, whenever possible, hold their hands to form a kind of basket. They must also allow the ball to settle in their hands softly. This is the best way to make a catch.

ends usually go over the middle and not as deep as the wide receivers. They are bigger and taller than the wide receivers because they have to block and catch passes in heavy traffic.

All pass receivers must practice their skills to become the best they can be. And they must start by learning to catch the football.

All good receivers have what is called "soft hands." This means their hands are relaxed, fingers spread and ready to let the ball settle into them. If the receiver fights the ball with his hands tight and tense, chances are he will drop it. No matter what kind

Receivers must be able to catch the ball while running full speed. The trick is to "look" the ball into the hands. This means the receiver should follow the ball at all times and always have those fingers spread to make the catch.

of ball he is trying to catch—high, low, over the head—soft, relaxed hands will make it much easier.

The receiver should practice by having someone throw the ball to him. He should relax his hands the second the ball hits them. Of course, in a game he will be catching the ball under very tough conditions. So besides soft hands, he will have to learn how to concentrate on the catch.

All good receivers know how to "look" the ball into their hands. That means they focus or concentrate on catching the pass

Sometimes a pass receiver must make a catch in heavy traffic, or with a defensive back hanging all over him. The same basic fundamentals apply. Watch the football and keep those fingers spread. Also, always try to catch the ball with both hands.

and nothing else. They can't worry about the defensive back running alongside them. Or, if they are going over the middle, they can't worry about being hit hard by a linebacker or safety. They must think of just one thing—catching the football. And to do that, the receiver has to watch the ball and nothing else.

This kind of concentration will help a receiver catch any kind of ball. Even if he has to leap or dive for it, he must focus and keep his hands spread and ready.

Once a receiver feels good about catching the ball, he should begin to work on his pass patterns. He will have to work with his coach and quarterback. The quarterback must know where his receiver is going to be on each play. That way he can find him quickly.

To get to where he should be, the receiver must develop his moves. He must be able to get past a defender so he will be in a good position to make the catch. If he doesn't do this, the defender may knock the ball away or even intercept it.

One move is a stop-and-go pattern. On this one, a receiver will run downfield and stop quickly. When the defender comes up on him, he will suddenly start again and burst past the defender into the clear. Another move is the buttonhook. On this one the receiver will run downfield, then hook around and come back to catch the ball.

Sometimes, a receiver will just fake to the inside as if he is going over the middle. Then he will cut back sharply toward the outside, or sideline. Other times he may do just the opposite. He may fake to the outside and come back over the middle. Very fast receivers will sometimes run a fly pattern. This means they will run downfield as fast as they can with no fakes. The object is to burst past the defenders for a long pass.

Each coach will teach the receiver different patterns. The receiver may even come up with some of his own. By working with his quarterback, he can try new things. A good quarterback and receiver are sometimes called a ''passing combination.''

Of course, after a receiver makes a catch, he can run with the ball. Then the receiver becomes just like a running back.

On still other plays, the receiver may have to block for a runner or other receiver. Here the rules for blocking will apply. So while a pass receiver must learn the special skills for his position, he still has to learn the general football skills needed to play an all-around game.

Learning To
Be A Lineman

There are both offensive and defensive linemen. They play across the line of scrimmage from each other and do battle for the entire game. Some people call it playing in the trenches. It is perhaps the toughest part of the game because linemen are banging each other on every single play.

Linemen have to have good size and strength. But they also have to be quick. Offensive linemen sometimes have to "pull" off the line and lead a runner around the end on a sweep. Defensive linemen have to be fast enough to rush the passer and quick enough to react to speedy ballcarriers coming through the holes.

All linemen must be strong enough not to be pushed off the play by the opponent across the line. Most linemen lift weights and do other exercises to become stronger and faster. Young people just beginning to play the game don't have to worry about becoming very big and strong right away. Coaches in Pop Warner and age group football try to keep their kids matched against others about the same size and weight.

As with the other positions, there are certain things all linemen must learn. So let's begin with blocking on the offensive line.

There are five offensive linemen—a center, two guards and two tackles. The center, of course, must snap the ball to the quarterback to start each play. All five linemen must block for running plays and protect the quarterback on pass plays.

Perhaps the most important thing for a linemen to have is strong legs. There are many exercises and drills to build up the legs. In practice, a group of linemen will push a blocking sled in order to build up their leg drive. This enables them to push or control the linemen working against them.

Along with good leg drive, linemen must learn basic blocking techniques. On certain plays, they will have to try to block their

Offensive linemen and blockers use several basic blocking techniques. One is the shoulder block. The blocker gets low and uses his shoulder and forearm to drive the defender back. Once the blocker makes contact, he uses his legs to drive into the player he is blocking. Offensive blockers cannot use their hands while making a block.

opponents in one direction or the other. To do this incorrectly could cause the play to fail.

Except for the center, a lineman usually gets in a three-point stance. He spreads his legs and gets down low, on one hand on the ground to keep him from falling forward. The other arm is held in front of his body, and he is balanced on the balls of his feet so he can push out hard. That first strong forward thrust right at the snap is very important.

If a lineman can block his opponent before the other man can make his move, there is a better chance the block will work. That's why quickness off the ball is so important.

This is the basic three-point stance used by linemen, running backs and some receivers. All players must learn to leap forward from this position. The linemen try to get power from their move. The backs and ends try for speed.

Blocking must be done from the front. To block a man from behind is a penalty. One of the basic blocks an offensive lineman uses is the shoulder block. To do this, he stays low and hits his opponent first with his shoulder and then drives with his legs in the direction he wants to move his man. The center, tackles or guards can also use their forearms to push opponents. But they cannot use their hands.

On running plays, the blocker should keep his head and body between his opponent and the ballcarrier. He should also keep his feet apart, so he will have good balance during the block. And he must continue to drive with his legs throughout the block.

A lineman can also use a side block, getting low and hitting his opponent with the side of his body. This block can be used to open a quick hole for a runner. Sometimes a blocker will roll into his opponent low, trying to knock him off his feet. But if he misses this block, he may not have a second chance.

Guards and tackles can use the basic shoulder block when they

On a side block, the blocker rolls into the defender using the side of his body to take the other player out of the play. Using a side block, a blocker can more easily knock his man off his feet. But if he misses the block, he may be out of position to recover.

get out in front of the ballcarrier on a sweep or end run. On a sweep, they sometimes have to take out just a single defender to clear the way for the runner, so the block should be a good one.

On pass blocking, the lineman will take several steps backward to form a pocket in front of the quarterback. They must then plant their feet, get down low and block the charging defenders straight on. They have to keep the defenders from getting past them and to the quarterback.

The defensive lineman has a slightly different job. But he must still be quick and strong and have a great deal of leg drive. In some defenses there are two defensive tackles and two defensive ends. Other defenses call for a single tackle and two defensive ends.

The job of the defensive tackle is to stop the run up the middle and to sometimes charge the quarterback. He must be able to fight off the block of the offensive lineman and hold his ground. To do this, he has to be very strong.

A defensive lineman must learn to fight off the blocks of the offensive players so he can tackle the ballcarrier. If he is blocked off the play, the runner may burst through the hole and go past him. A defensive lineman must also have very strong arms and shoulders in order to stop a back who is running at full speed.

Defensive linemen are allowed to use their hands to push and pull the offensive lineman. This is one difference. But like the offensive linemen, they must be quick off the ball and hit their man first. That way, they will be less likely to be moved off the play.

Defensive ends have to guard against sweeps to the outside and are also the primary pass rushers on the line. Speed is very important to a defensive end. But he must also be able to fight off blocks and develop his own moves. Sometimes a defensive end will try to spin away from a tackle's block. Other times he will just

Speed is very important to a defensive back. He is a smaller player who is quick enough to cover pass receivers and tackle ballcarriers in the open field. A defensive back sometimes has to catch a runner or receiver from behind, and he must still be able to make the tackle.

try to use his speed to go around the blocker. And sometimes a defensive end will jump over a blocker who is down too low.

All defenders must be able to tackle the ballcarrier. Strong arms are a big help in tackling. Sometimes a defensive lineman will just grab a runner and throw him to the ground. He can also hit him low and try to knock the runner's legs out from under him. A defender can also roll into a runner and knock him down.

A young person playing football for the first time may find himself going both ways. So if he plays the line on both offense and defense, he will have to learn how to block on one side of the line and fight off blocks on the other. And that can only make him a better football player.

Learning To Be
A Linebacker

Linebackers play a big role in a team's defense. It isn't an easy position to play. A linebacker must be strong enough to jump into the line of scrimmage and rush the passer. He must also be tough enough to help make tackles in the middle. But he also has to have enough speed to cover pass receivers and chase runners on sweeps.

A linebacker must really have all the skills of playing defense. Most times he starts a few feet behind the line of scrimmage. But on some plays, one or two linebackers may get down to a three-point stance right beside the linemen.

Some teams have a middle linebacker and two outside linebackers. In other defenses, there are two inside linebackers and two outside linebackers. The middle and inside linebackers are usually a little bigger and better at stopping the run. The outside linebackers should have a little more speed and be able to cover pass receivers or backs going out for a pass.

A linebacker should also be in tip-top condition. He will be doing a lot of running during a game and also a lot of hard-hitting. He can work with the linemen on learning how to fight off blocks and with the defensive backs on covering passes. He must practice his tackling. Good linebackers always make a lot of tackles.

A linebacker has a great deal to learn. He must follow the game plan carefully and let his coach tell him what area of the field he has to cover on each play.

Learning To Be
A Defensive Back

Defensive backs are not usually very big, but they must be fast. In most defenses there are four defensive backs. Two are called cornerbacks. They play to the outside of and behind the linebackers and cover the wide receivers. The other two defensive backs are called safeties. They are the last line of defense and line up toward the middle of the field.

The *strong* safety is usually the biggest defensive back because he often has to cover the tight end. The *free* safety helps out wherever he is needed. Sometimes he will sneak up to the line and rush the quarterback. Other times he will double up or help a cornerback cover a wide receiver. And still other times he's busy tackling ballcarriers.

All defensive backs must be fast and quick. It also helps if they can jump high, as they will often be battling tall receivers for passes. Cornerbacks, especially, must work very hard on man-to-man coverage of pass receivers.

It isn't easy for a defensive back to cover a speedy wide receiver. To begin with, the defender is often moving backwards, and once he is faked out, it is hard for him to recover. If he loses just a split second because of a fake, the pass may be completed. Defensive backs should practice backpedaling quickly and changing direction. They must also take crossover steps when running backwards and cannot afford to let their legs get tangled.

A defensive back should always watch the middle of the receiver's chest. If he watches his head or feet, he may easily fall for a fake. He must also try to stay alongside the receiver or in a position where he can either knock the ball away or intercept it. Timing is very important.

A defensive back can go for the football, or he can hit the re-

The defensive back must be able to knock a pass away from a receiver at just the right time. If the defender hits the receiver too soon, it results in a penalty, which gives the other team a first down. He must learn to make his move just as the receiver tries to catch the football.

ceiver as soon as the ball arrives. But he cannot push the receiver out of the way or try to keep him from catching the ball by holding his arms. The defensive back is not permitted to block the receiver's vision so he cannot see the pass coming.

These last three things will result in pass-interference penalties and will give the offensive team a first down at the point of the foul. So defensive backs try to avoid this penalty.

Cornerbacks and safeties must also make open-field tackles. If they are one-on-one with a ballcarrier, they must not fall for fakes. Instead, they must try to hit the ballcarrier just above the knee area and drive him to the ground. A smaller defensive back should not try to tackle a larger ballcarrier by the arms or shoulders. He may find himself left in the dust if he does that.

A defensive back must also be able to bounce back. If he is beaten by a receiver for a long gain or a touchdown, everyone watching will know it. The defensive back cannot let that affect the rest of his game. He must play tough, determined to stop his opponent the next time.

If a defensive back should intercept a pass, he then becomes a runner and tries to bring the ball back upfield. Then, all the skills of the running game apply to him. Defensive backs do a great deal of running during a game and must always be in top condition.

No matter what position a young person plays, it is important to remember one thing above all. Football is a team game. The offensive and defensive teams must work together. No one player is going to win or lose a game. The way a player can help the most is to learn his position thoroughly and always do the very best job he can.

Learning The Kicking Game

There are two types of kicks used during a football game. One is the placekick for kicking off, extra points and field goals. The other is the punt, used to put the ball deeper into the opponent's territory. Kickers must work very hard at their skills. Games can be won or lost by a good or bad kick. Most pro teams today have a player who only placekicks and another who only punts.

Both placekickers and punters must perform under a lot of pressure. Late in the game, both types of kickers can be very important. Anytime they kick, there are defenders charging at them, screaming and trying to block the kick. A good kicker will shut all this out. He will focus on the mechanics of his kick and nothing else. All good kickers have the ability to concentrate this way.

On most placekicks, the ball is kicked directly off the ground. But it is kicked from a tee on kickoffs. For extra points and field goals, the ball is snapped to a holder who waits on one knee. He then places it straight up on the ground as the kicker steps forward and boots it. It takes perfect timing between the snapper, the holder and the kicker to execute a placekick.

There are two ways to placekick. One is the straight ahead style. The kicker stands directly behind the ball and swings his leg straight through it. The second is soccer style or sidewinding. In this style, the kicker stands to the right or left of the ball, and when he steps up to kick, he swings his leg across at an angle and kicks the ball with his instep instead of his toe. Most kickers today use the soccer style to placekick.

With either style, there are some basic rules to follow. The holder will set up on one knee about seven yards behind the line of scrimmage. The kicker is several yards behind him. When the kicker is ready, he just watches the holder and the spot where the ball will be placed. At the snap, he begins his kicking motion.

He will take one short step with his kicking leg, then a longer step with his nonkicking leg. He will then plant his foot and swing his leg into the ball. He has to shut out everything else but the kick. His kicking motion must always be the same, whether he is trying an extra point or a long field goal. As he swings his leg

Most placekickers today use the soccer style of kicking. This means they approach the ball from an angle and swing the instep of their foot into it. The old, straight-ahead kickers used their toe. The placekicker also must have perfect timing with the center and his holder, who places the ball on a kicking block just as he steps into it. This kind of timing takes many hours of practice.

into the ball, he must keep his head down until he has completed the kick. If he raises his head too quickly, he may well ruin the kick.

The kicker must get the ball in the air quickly. If he kicks too low, it will be blocked by a lineman or other defender who may be leaping high in the air. Defenders cannot hit a kicker. If they do, there is a roughing penalty and the offensive team gets 15 yards and another down.

Punters cannot be hit either. They stand about 15 yards behind the line of scrimmage but do not kick the ball while it is on the ground. Instead, they hold the ball and drop it in front of them, kicking it with the instep of their foot before it hits the ground.

Once the punter catches the ball from the center, he takes two steps forward, then gets ready to drop the ball onto his foot.

A good punter will kick very high. That way his team has a chance to get downfield and stop a return. And there are some rules every punter must follow. The punter should move his leg straight through the ball with his knee locked and his toe pointed straight outward. Leg strength and speed are very important. The more leg speed, the longer the punt will be. The follow-through should be made with the head down and leg continuing up to head level or higher.

The punter must also have good hands in order to catch the ball from the snapper. If the snap is to the left or right, the punter

As he begins to swing his kicking leg upward, the punter releases the ball so that his foot makes contact when the ball is at just the right angle. The instep of the foot, not the point of the toe, should make contact with the ball.

should try to move his whole body in front of it. He should not reach out for it and then try to square up his body again.

The steps are very similar to the placekick: one short step with the kicking leg, then a long step to plant the nonkicking foot, drop the ball and boom! It's not a long drop. In fact, the punter almost places the ball on his foot. He drops it tilted slightly toward the ground and slightly angled toward the nonkicking leg. If hit right, the kick will spiral.

Punters don't always boom the ball as far as they can. A punt going into the end zone is brought out to the 20-yard line. So a

The punter must be sure to follow through. This means continuing the leg swing until the foot is almost level with the head. The punter must also keep his eye on the ball and not lift his head too soon. If he lifts his head too soon, he probably will not kick the ball well.

good punter will practice "angling" the ball out of bounds inside the 20. If the ball goes out at the seven-yard line, for example, the referee will place it at the seven.

The kickoff is used at the beginning of the game and at the start of the second half. It is also used after touchdowns and field goals to put the ball back into play. Kickoffs take place from the 40-yard line with the ball placed on a tee.

The kickoff style is the same as for field goals and extra points. The only difference is that the kicker has no one charging him. So he can take a few extra steps when he approaches the ball. That way he can kick it even further and help his team get a better field position.

Obviously, there is a great deal of skill needed to punt and placekick. To become good takes many, many hours of practice, good work habits and the desire to succeed. So if a young player wants to be a kicker, he had better start working hard right now.

A Little More
About the Game

Not everyone on a football team starts on offense or defense. Some players are members of the special teams. This means they play on kickoffs and punts, or kickoff and punt returns. In the National Football League, special teams were once known as "suicide squads" because of the way the players ran at each other at top speed.

Special teams are very important to the success of a football team. A player who is a member of the kickoff team must still play hard and listen to his coach. He must also be a good open-field tackler and a good blocker, and he can't worry about being hurt.

Playing on special teams takes many of the same skills as playing on offense or defense. And if he works hard as a member of a special team, a young player may find himself in the regular lineup before very long.

Most teams come into a contest with a set "game plan." The game plan is made by the coaching staff. If the team has a really good quarterback and receivers, its game plan may call for a lot of passing. If the team has one or two very good running backs, then the game plan may be to run the football.

Most teams use a number of different offensive and defensive "sets." A set is how the team lines up to begin a play. Since the defense must adjust to the offense, a defense team must be ready for nearly any look, or set, an offense gives them.

Most pro offenses start with a quarterback, two running backs, two wide receivers and a tight end. But some formations call for three wide receivers and one running back. A few teams have an offense with two big tight ends. It all depends on the opponent. A team will often change its look a number of times during a game.

The pro set formation has the two running backs split behind the quarterback, one to the right and one to the left. But the I formation has the two runners directly behind the quarterback in the straight line. In the "shotgun" formation, the quarterback stands about six yards behind the center and takes a direct snap. This formation is usually used when a team has to pass.

Defenses also change during a game. Some pro teams start with four defensive linemen and three linebackers. Others use three linemen and four linebackers. But there are times when five linebackers are in the game. On certain passing situations, a fifth defensive back (called the "nickle" back) comes into the game.

Coaches are always trying to out-think each other. They may have a couple of trick plays to use during a game. Or, if they think their opponents are looking for a lot of passing, they may try to run more. Strategy plays a big part in football. The longer a person plays, the more he will learn about it.

One more thing. Since football is such a hard-hitting game, it must be watched closely. There are seven officials at college and pro games. Officials always wear black-and-white striped shirts and are sometimes called "zebras."

The head official is called the referee. He makes the final decision on all calls and uses a series of hand signals to indicate penalties, scores, time-outs and everything else. The referee in pro games has a microphone on his belt and can also announce his calls.

Other officials are called the umpire, the head linesman, the line judge, the back judge, the field judge and the side judge.

Learning to play the game correctly is very important. All the players must know the fundamentals of their positions. They must also follow their coaches' game plans. The result of all this is the fun of playing the game well and maybe being part of the winning touchdown. That's the greatest feeling of all for any football player.

Each has a special area of the field and the game to watch. With all these officials, it is very difficult for any player to break the rules without being seen. And because there are so many officials, most football games are kept under control. There are very few real fights.

If a young person thinks he will like the game of football, he should begin to play early. He should find a team with a good coach and start to learn the game the right way. Then he'll know if he wants to keep playing or not.

If he wants to keep playing, he should learn all he can about the sport and the different positions. That way he can decide where he wants to play. If he wants to be a quarterback, a linebacker or a placekicker, he will know what it takes to play each position. And if he starts with the basics and learns as much as he can about the game, then he can be a better player. And that's always what every athlete wants.

Glossary

Blitz   Play in which a number of defensive players (linebackers and defensive backs) rush the quarterback instead of covering their normal defensive positions.

Crossbar   The horizontal part of the goalpost. The ball must pass over it for an extra point or field goal attempt to be good.

Cut, or **Cutback**   A quick change of direction by a ballcarrier in an attempt to avoid a tackler.

Down   Term used to number the plays during a football game. An offensive team has four downs in which to make ten yards. If they make the ten yards or more on any down, they begin over again with another first down.

Dropback   The quick retreat of a quarterback who is getting ready to throw a forward pass. Quarterbacks usually drop back about seven yards to give their receivers time to get downfield.

End Zone   The ten-yard area beyond each goal line in which a touchdown can be scored. Teams can advance the ball into the end zone by running or passing.

Extra Point   After each touchdown, there is a chance for an additional point. Teams usually placekick for the point, though they may also run or pass for it. In college ball, a run or pass counts two extra points.

Field Goal   A field goal counts three points and is made when the offensive team place kicks the ball through the goalposts and over the crossbar.

Fumble   The dropping of the football by an offensive player during a play. The ''free'' ball can then be recovered by either team.

Handoff   The exchange of the football between the quarterback and a running back. The quarterback literally hands the ball off to the back as he runs past him.

Huddle   A circle of offensive players back from the line of scrimmage in which the team calls the next play.

Line of Scrimmage   Whenever the football is placed on the field, an imaginary line runs from both sides of the ball to the sidelines. It divides the offensive team from the defensive unit.

Nickel Back   An extra defensive back put into the game in certain passing situations, usually when there is an extra pass receiver in the offensive lineup.

Option Play   Name given to a play in which the quarterback has a choice whether to run or pass.

Passing Combination   Term used to describe a quarterback and pass receiver who work very well together.

61

Penalty A loss of yardage by either team caused by a violation of the rules.

Pitchout A play in which the quarterback pitches the ball underhanded to a running back who is perhaps five yards from him, too far away to take a handoff.

Placekick Term given to a kickoff, field goal or extra point attempt when the ball is kicked while being held on the ground or sitting on a kicking tee.

Pocket A circle of blockers surrounding the quarterback to protect him from defenders after he has dropped back to pass.

Pro Set An offensive formation with two running backs split several feet apart behind the quarterback.

Punt A type of kick used to get the football downfield, usually when the offensive team has a fourth down deep in its down territory. The punter takes a long snap from center and boots the ball before it hits the ground.

Read To know what kind of play is coming before it happens. Both offensive and defensive players can ''read'' each other by watching formations and player movement carefully.

Return A term used to describe carrying the football after it has been exchanged on a kickoff, punt, interception or fumble recovery. The return is part of the same play in which the ball changed hands.

Safety A score counting two points and occurring when a member of the offensive team is tackled with the football in his own end zone.

Shotgun An offensive formation in which the quarterback stands perhaps five or six yards behind the center and takes a direct snap. It is generally used in passing situations.

Snap Term used to describe the underleg pass from the center to quarterback, center to punter, or center to the holder for a placekick.

Special Teams Players who are on the kickoff, kickoff return, punt and punt return units. Some players who are on the regular offensive and defensive units also play on special teams.

Suicide Squads A nickname given to special teams because of the hard hitting and full speed collisions during kicks and kick returns.

Three-Point Stance The starting position for most linemen before a play. The player squats down low, feet spread apart, with his weight balanced on the one arm that touches the ground. The two feet and the hand on the ground make the three points.

Touchdown The best way to score in football. Worth six points, a touchdown is scored by running or throwing the ball into the end zone.

Zebras Nickname given to the on-field officials because of the traditional black-and-white striped shirts they always wear.